At Sylvan, we believe anyone can master math skills and develop a love of reading, and we are glad you have chosen our resources to help your children experience the joy of both subjects as they build crucial reasoning skills. We know that time spent reinforcing lessons learned in school will contribute to understanding and mastery.

Reading comprehension is the foundation of success in all aspects of second-grade academics. As a successful reader, you hold infinite possibilities in your hands, enabling you to learn about anything and everything. Similarly, success in math requires more than just memorizing basic facts and algorithms; it also requires children to make connections between the real world and math concepts in order to solve problems. Successful problem solvers will be ready for the challenges of mathematics as they advance to more complex topics and encounter new problems both in school and at home.

We use a research-based, step-by-step process in teaching both reading and math that includes thought-provoking reading selections, math problems, and activities. The learning process also relies on high standards and meaningful parental involvement. With success, students feel increasing confidence. With increasing confidence, students build even more success. It's a perfect cycle. That's why our Sylvan workbooks aren't like the others. We're laying out the roadmap for learning that is designed to lead your child to success in school.

Included with your purchase of this workbook is a coupon for a discount at a participating Sylvan center. We hope you will use this coupon to further your children's academic journeys. Let us partner with you to support the development of confident, well-prepared, independent learners.

The Sylvan Team

2nd Grade
Reading & Math
Workout

Copyright © 2014 by Sylvan Learning, Inc.

All rights reserved.

Published in the United States by Random House LLC, New York, and in Canada by Random House of Canada Limited, Toronto.

A Penguin Random House Company.

www.tutoring.sylvanlearning.com

Created by Smarterville Productions LLC
Producer: TJ Trochlil McGreevy
Producer & Editorial Direction: The Linguistic Edge
Writers: Amy Kraft and Christina Wilsdon
Cover and Interior Illustrations: Shawn Finley and Duendes del Sur
Layout and Art Direction: SunDried Penguin
Art Manager: Adina Ficano
Director of Product Development: Russell Ginns

First Edition

ISBN: 978-1-101-88189-7

Library of Congress Cataloging-in-Publication Data available upon request.

This book is available at special discounts for bulk purchases for sales promotions or premiums. For more information, write to Special Markets/Premium Sales, 1745 Broadway, MD 6-2, New York, New York 10019 or e-mail specialmarkets@randomhouse.com.

PRINTED IN CHINA

10 9 8 7 6 5 4 3 2 1

2nd Grade
Reading Skill Builders

2nd Grade
Reading Skill Builders

Contents

Blend Two Consonants

Sort It Out

What do you call a blend of two consonants? A **consonant blend**, of course! Each letter makes its own sound but also blends with its buddy's sound, as in words like *fly*, *plate*, and *train*.

SORT the words. PUT the words into the lists. WRITE them on the blanks.

flip	break	cloud	black	grape	clam	blue	green
clock	block	bring	flower	brave	ground	floppy	

br

_____   _____   _____

_____   _____   _____

_____   _____   _____

cl

fl

gr

_____   _____

_____   _____

_____   _____

bl

Herd That Word

Yee-haw! Cowgirl Kris has to round up words with the right consonant blends. Help her find them!

LOOK at the blend next to each fence. READ the words inside the fence. CIRCLE the word that starts with the correct blend.

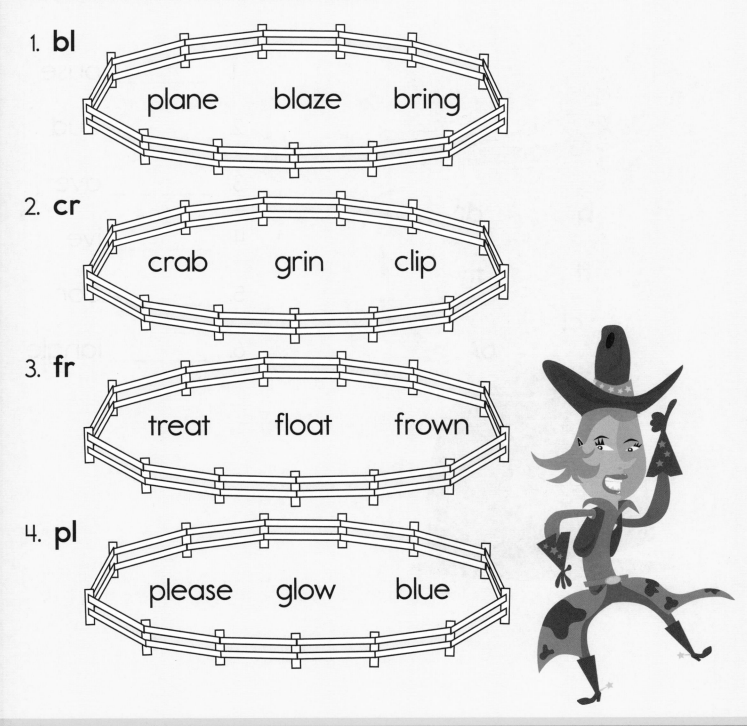

1. **bl**

plane   blaze   bring

2. **cr**

crab   grin   clip

3. **fr**

treat   float   frown

4. **pl**

please   glow   blue

Blender Blunder

Uh-oh! Somebody spilled words into the blender. They got chopped up. Can you put them back together?

LOOK at the consonant blends in the blender. MATCH each blend with the right ending. FILL IN the blanks with the correct blends.

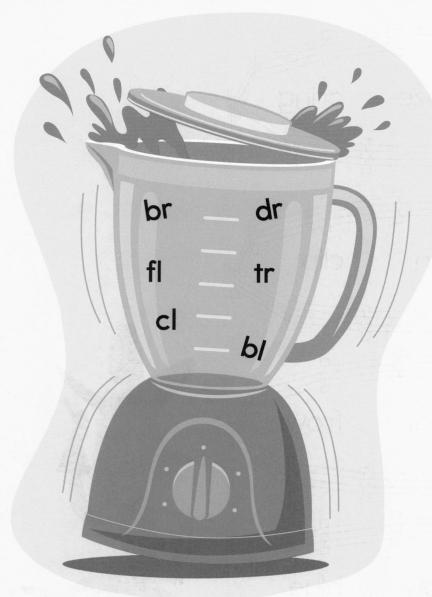

1. _____ ouse

2. _____ oud

3. _____ ave

4. _____ ive

5. _____ oor

6. _____ iangle

You've Got Mail

The letter "s" is friends with many consonants. It's in the blends missing from this e-mail.

LOOK at the consonant blends word box. FILL IN the blanks with the right blends. You can use blends more than once.

sc	sk	sl	sm	sn	sp	st	sw

Wow! Today I flew down a _____eep hill on my

_____ateboard. I went so fast, the wheels made _____oke.

It was _____eet! But I had to _____ow down and _____in

sideways when a _____unk suddenly crawled across the

street like a tired _____ail, or else it would have made a big

_____ink. _____ary!

Who Says?

Yakkity-yak! Who's saying that?

READ each sentence. CIRCLE the beginning blends that repeat three times in each sentence. MATCH sentences with names. DRAW lines between them.

HINT: Each speaker uses three words with blends that match the blend in his or her name.

1. I'm (cr)abby because a (cr)ocodile ate my (cr)ayon.

2. There's a spot of spinach on my spoon.

3. I ate a snack and made a snake snowman.

4. My frog likes French fries.

5. A troll on a tractor is trouble.

6. Please don't put your plant on my plate.

Trixie

Francis

Craig

Snowden

Placido

Spencer

Sound Search

OK, detective. Track down consonant blends in this story.

READ the story. CIRCLE each word that starts with a consonant blend. FILL IN the blanks with the words.

The people of France couldn't sleep because a creepy dragon prowled the land. It crushed houses every night. Its claws broke branches off trees. Its breath fried the grass. What a problem!

One night, it tried to trap the prince. But then it yelped and flew away. "It's scared of me," said a grinning spider sitting on the ground nearby. "Pretty great!"

You've Got Mail

Some blends are made up of three consonant sounds. The letter "s" pops up a lot, as in *spread*, *square*, and *stroke*.

LOOK at the consonant blends in the word box. FILL IN the blanks in the e-mail with the right blends. You can use blends more than once.

scr	spl	squ	str

A really _____ange thing happened today. I was eating a

bowl of _____awberry ice cream when I heard a loud

_____eech. Then I heard a _____eak and a _____awk.

I jumped up to look out the window and saw a noisy

_____uggle going on between a _____irrel and a bird. They

were playing tug-of-war with a _____ing! Suddenly the bird

let go. The _____uirrel fell into the _____eam with a _____ash.

I sat down in surprise. Whoops. I _____ashed

my ice cream—and let out a _____eam!

Sort It Out

SORT the words. PUT the words into the lists.

square	stripe	squash	screech	spray	split	scram	strike
spread	street	splat	spring	squirm	scream	splash	

spr

_____

_____

_____

squ

_____

_____

_____

spl

_____

_____

_____

scr

_____

_____

_____

str

_____

_____

_____

End with a Blend

Herd That Word

Words sometimes end with consonant blends, as in *elf*, *pump*, and *bent*. Cowgirl Pearl is busy rounding up some correct blends at the end of words!

LOOK at the blend next to each fence. READ the words inside the fence. CIRCLE the word that ends with the correct blend.

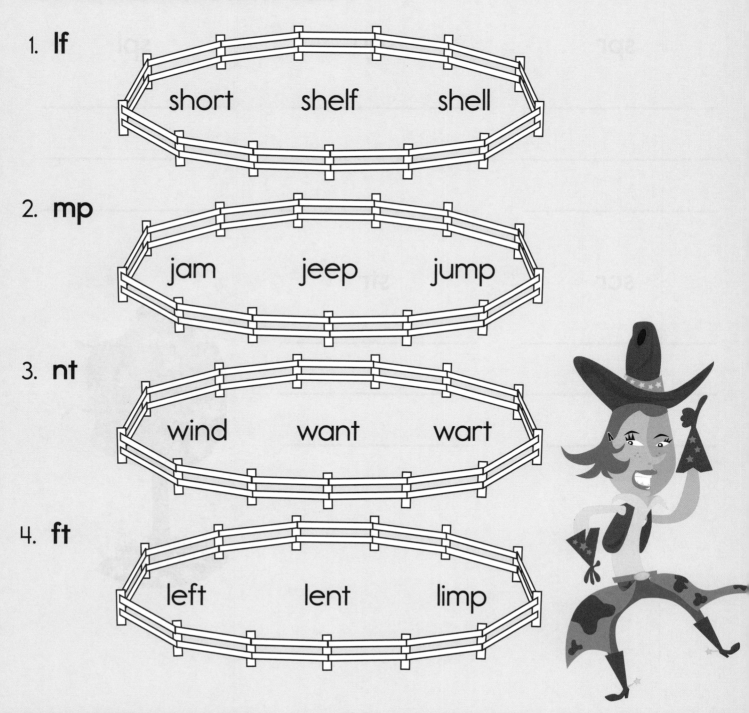

1. **lf**

short   shelf   shell

2. **mp**

jam   jeep   jump

3. **nt**

wind   want   wart

4. **ft**

left   lent   limp

Who Says?

READ each sentence. CIRCLE the final blends that repeat three times in each sentence. MATCH sentences with names. DRAW lines between them.

HINT: Each sentence has three words that end with the same blend. Each name ends in a blend too.

1. The wind blew my towel and hat off the sand.

   Hank

2. Honk if you'd like a pink tank!

   Millicent

3. I did not need a potato, but my aunt went and sent me one.

   Fisk

4. I saw her jump off the ramp into the swamp.

   Desmond

5. The best horses in the West run fast.

   Amethyst

6. Ask the elephant to do the task with its tusk.

   Kemp

Blender Blunder

LOOK at the final blends in the blender. MATCH each blend with the right beginning.
FILL IN the blanks with the correct blends.

ft

nt

mp

lt

st

nk

1. breakfa_____

2. so_____

3. se_____

4. fe_____

5. su_____

6. swa_____

What's This?

LOOK at each picture. READ the words next to it. CIRCLE the correct word.

HINT: Keep an eye on those end blends!

1. lamp   land   last

2. art   and   ant

3. deep   desk   dent

4. end   ear   elf

Sort It Out

The words in the box contain consonant blends. Some words start with two-letter blends. Others start with three-letter blends. Some have blends at the end.

SORT the words. PUT the words into the lists.

cry	sink	wind	string	sting	stone
scratch	sand	street	screech	junk	creep

Beginning

cr

_____

_____

st

_____

_____

scr

_____

_____

str

_____

_____

End

nk

_____

_____

nd

_____

_____

Match the Socks

What a mess! Can you match up these socks?

READ the words on the socks. MATCH each sock with another sock that contains a word with the same blend. COLOR the socks so they match.

HINT: Socks match if they start or end with the same blends.

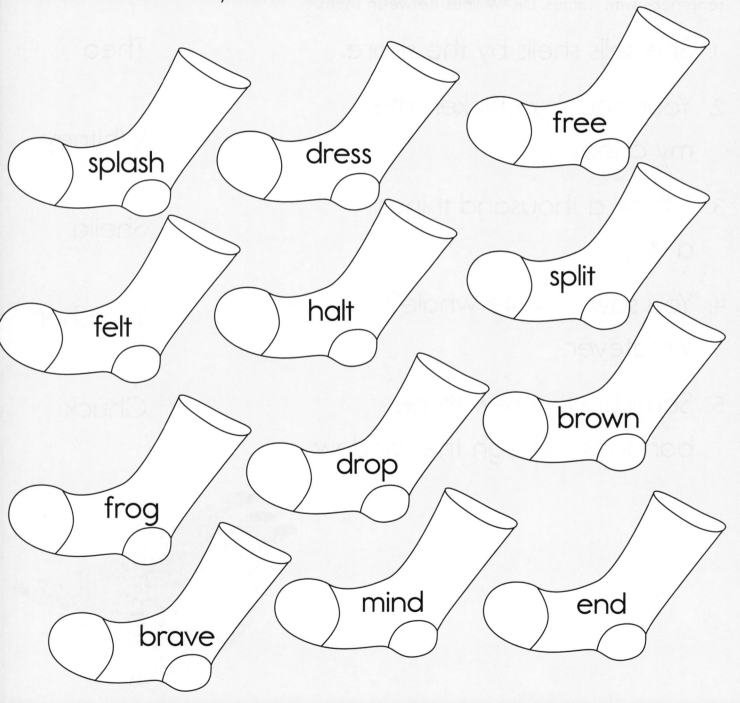

splash

dress

free

felt

halt

split

frog

drop

brown

brave

mind

end

Consonant Combos

Who Says?

Some consonant letters pair up to make a whole new sound, as in *cheer*, *fish*, and *thump*. We call these teams **consonant combos**. Check these chats for consonant combos. Each name shares a combo with one sentence.

READ each sentence. CIRCLE the consonant combos that repeat three times. MATCH sentences with names. DRAW lines between them.

1. She sells shells by the shore.

2. Your chubby chicken ate my cheese.

3. I think a thousand things a day.

4. You saw a white whale? Whatever.

5. Somebody threw three bananas through the window.

Theo

Whitney

Sheila

Thrasher

Chuck

Blender Blunder

LOOK at the consonant combos in the blender. MATCH each consonant combo with the right ending. FILL IN the blanks with the correct consonant combos.

sh
ch
th
thr
wh

1. _____eese

2. _____eel

3. _____under

4. _____ead

5. _____ark

Herd That Word

The consonant combo "ng" sounds like the "ing" in *bring* when it's at the end of a word. The consonant combo "gh" often sounds like f at a word's end. Help Cowgirl Spring look for words that end in these consonant combos.

LOOK at the consonant combo next to each fence. READ the words inside the fence. CIRCLE the word that ends with the correct combo.

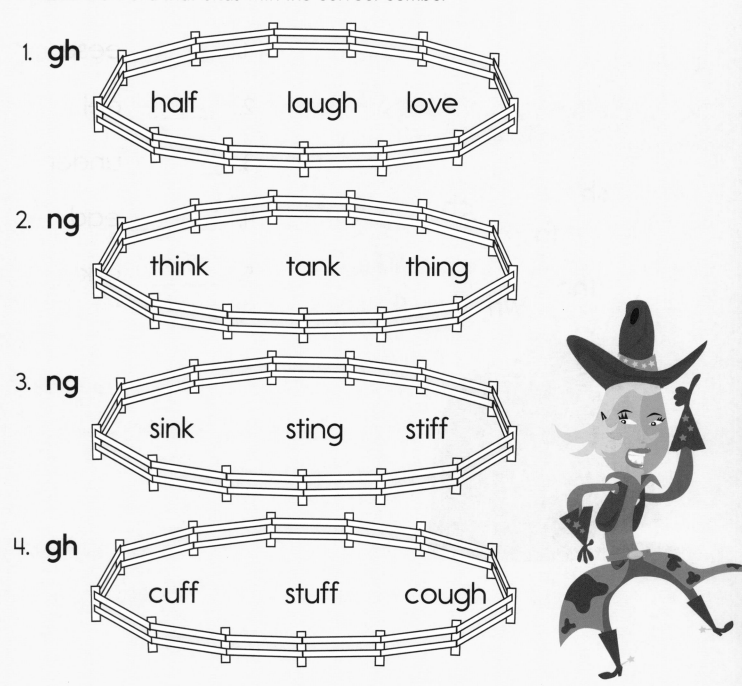

1. **gh**

   half   laugh   love

2. **ng**

   think   tank   thing

3. **ng**

   sink   sting   stiff

4. **gh**

   cuff   stuff   cough

Say Hey!

READ the sentences. FILL IN the blanks with words from the word box.

HINT: Each missing word contains a consonant combo and rhymes with a word next to it in the sentence.

laugh	sting	tough	rang	song	rough

1. A piece of sandpaper is _____ stuff!

2. Does that buzzing thing _____?

3. That's only a little funny, so I'll just half _____.

4. The singer sang a very, very long _____.

5. Then he took out bells and _____, sang, and danced!

6. That rope will break because it's

   not _____ enough.

Hard or Soft?

Sound Search

The letter "c" can sound like either **k** or **s**. Hard "c" sounds like **k**, as in *cold*. Soft "c" sounds like **s**, as in *cent*. "C" if you can find them in this story!

READ the story. CIRCLE words that start with hard "c." DRAW a line under words that start with soft "c." FILL IN the blanks with the words.

Sassy the dog followed the tracks of Cinnamon the cat into a cave. A cold wind blew. Cobwebs hung from the ceiling. Centipedes ran across the floor. Suddenly she heard "meow" . . . and "tweet"! There in the center of a circle of rocks was the kitty—with a stolen canary!

Hard c   Soft c

_____   _____

_____   _____

_____   _____

_____   _____

Follow That Sound

START at the arrow. DRAW a line along the path that is lined with words that start with a hard "c" to get to the cupcake.

Sort It Out

The letter "g" can be hard or soft too. A hard "g" sounds like the **g** in *goose*. A soft "g" sounds like **j**, as in *gem*.

SORT the words. PUT the words into the lists.

gab	giant	general	game	giraffe	garden
gobble	goat	gentle	germ	girl	ginger

Hard g   Soft g

_____   _____

_____   _____

_____   _____

_____   _____

_____   _____

Herd That Word

Giddy-up! Cowgirl Gina has a hard job, but she's no softie. Gee-haw!

LOOK at the "g" next to each fence. READ the words inside the fence. CIRCLE the word that starts with the correct sound.

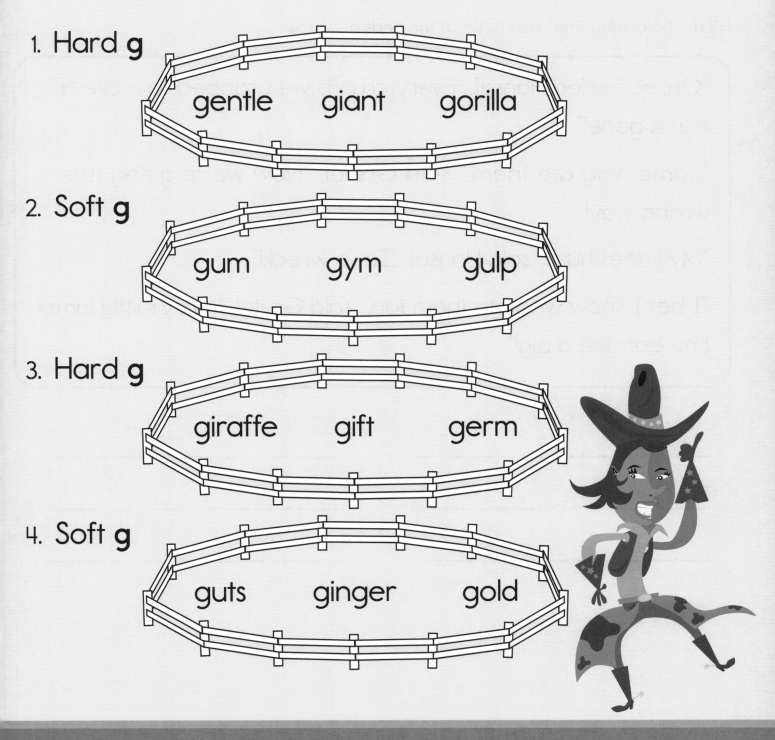

1. Hard **g**

gentle   giant   gorilla

2. Soft **g**

gum   gym   gulp

3. Hard **g**

giraffe   gift   germ

4. Soft **g**

guts   ginger   gold

23

Sound Search

You can see them, but you can't hear them! They're letters in the **silent** consonant combos "kn," "wr," and "mb." The "k," "w," and "b" don't make a peep. See if you can find words with silent consonant combos in this story.

READ the story. CIRCLE words with silent consonant combos. FILL IN the blanks with the words.

HINT: The combo "mb" likes to be at the ends of words.

"Oh, no!" cried Hansel. "Every crumb we dropped to make a trail is gone!"

"Something ate them," said Gretel. "Now we're going the wrong way!"

"My knees hurt," said Hansel. "I'm a wreck!"

"I bet I know who ate them too," said Gretel. "Mary's little lamb! She eats like a pig!"

_____   _____

_____   _____

_____

What's This?

LOOK at each picture. READ the words next to it. CIRCLE the correct word.

HINT: *Shh!* The correct word has a silent consonant combo in it!

1. night   knight   knot

2. come   cob   comb

3. writer   water   wrong

4. nee   knee   kneel

Match the Socks

READ the words on the socks. MATCH each sock with another sock that contains a word with the same sound. COLOR the socks so they match.

HINT: Socks match if they start or end with the same consonant combo or blend.

Who Says?

READ each sentence. CIRCLE the beginning or ending sounds that repeat three times in each sentence. MATCH sentences with names. DRAW lines between them.

HINT: Each speaker uses three words that share a sound with his or her name.

1. That goofy goat ate my soccer gear.

   Carl

2. I can't carry your camel today.

   Cindy

3. Wrap the box and write "wrong address" on it.

   Shelby

4. The shark has sharp teeth, but don't worry—it's shy.

   Hough

5. I cough when I laugh hard enough.

   Wren

6. The circus is coming to Centipede City!

   Gordon

Build It

The letter "e" is powerful when it's at the end of a word. It can change the word's sound by making its vowel long! *Hat*, for example, turns into *hate*.

ADD a final "e" to each word. FILL IN the blanks with the new words.

1. cut   + e = _____

2. dim   + e = _____

3. fin   + e = _____

4. fir   + e = _____

5. kit   + e = _____

6. mad + e = _____

7. pin   + e = _____

8. plan + e = _____

Sound Search

READ the story. CIRCLE the words that have a final "e" that makes another vowel long. FILL IN the blanks with the words.

A mole stuck its nose out of the ground.

"Looks fine, Elly," he said.

Elly came out too. "I hate the sun," she said, blinking.

So they crawled to the shade of a pine by the lake. Suddenly a scary shape flew over—but it was just a plane. Then another scary thing appeared—but it was just a kite.

But the third time, Zak shouted, "Hide! Dive into the hole!"

"How rude," said the mule. "I just wanted to tell them a joke."

Yo, Poet!

The letter "a" in *same* is a long vowel. But vowels can team up to sound like **a** too. These teams include "ei," "ai," and "ay."

READ the poem. FILL IN the blanks with long **a** words from the word box.

pain	play	wail	way	eight
gray	jail	pails	rain	

The sky was dark. The clouds were _____.
₁

Can I go out and _____? No _____!
₂   ₃

I don't want to get wet in the _____.
₄

What a bummer! What a _____!
₅

I feel like I am locked in _____.
₆

I want to cry and moan and _____.
₇

And fill ten _____ with all my tears.
₈

I bet it pours for _____ more years.
₉

Follow That Sound

START at the arrow. DRAW a line along the path filled with words that have a long **a** sound to get to the amazing brain.

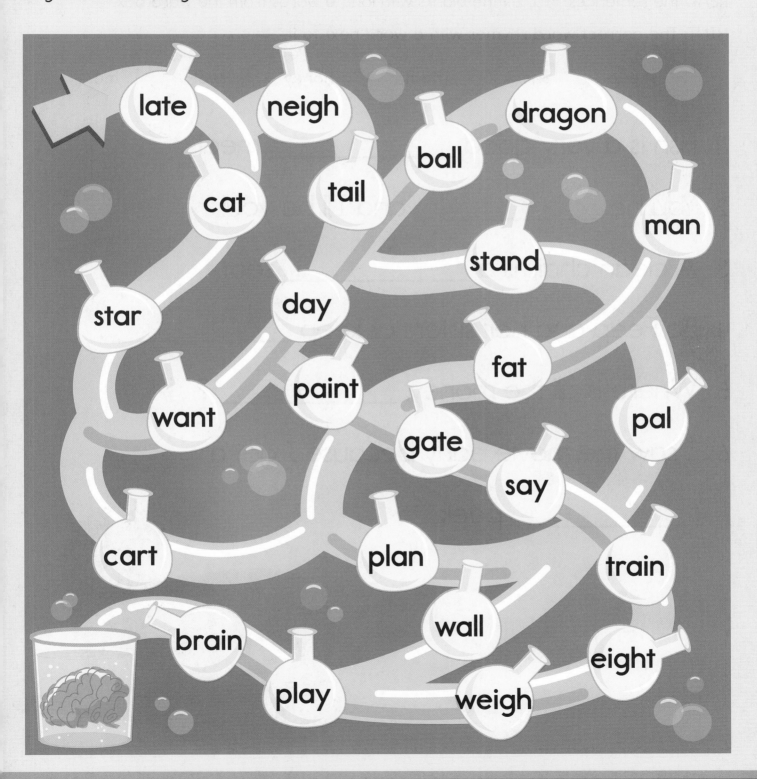

Say Hey!

See an "e," "ea," "ee," or "ey," and you may hear long **e**!

READ the sentences. FILL IN the blanks with long **e** words from the word box.

HINT: The correct word rhymes with a word next to it.

sheep	sneak	neat	honey	seal	me

1. Fish is a very good _____ meal.

2. You be _____ and I'll be you!

3. A clean chair is a _____ seat.

4. Bo Peep and her sisters all keep _____.

5. Where is all the money, _____?

6. I saw the movie early because I got a _____ peek.

Herd That Word

Yee-haw! Long **e** can't flee when it's seen by Cowgirl Jean.

LOOK at the spelling of the long **e** sound next to each fence. READ the words inside the fence. CIRCLE the word that has the correct spelling of long **e**.

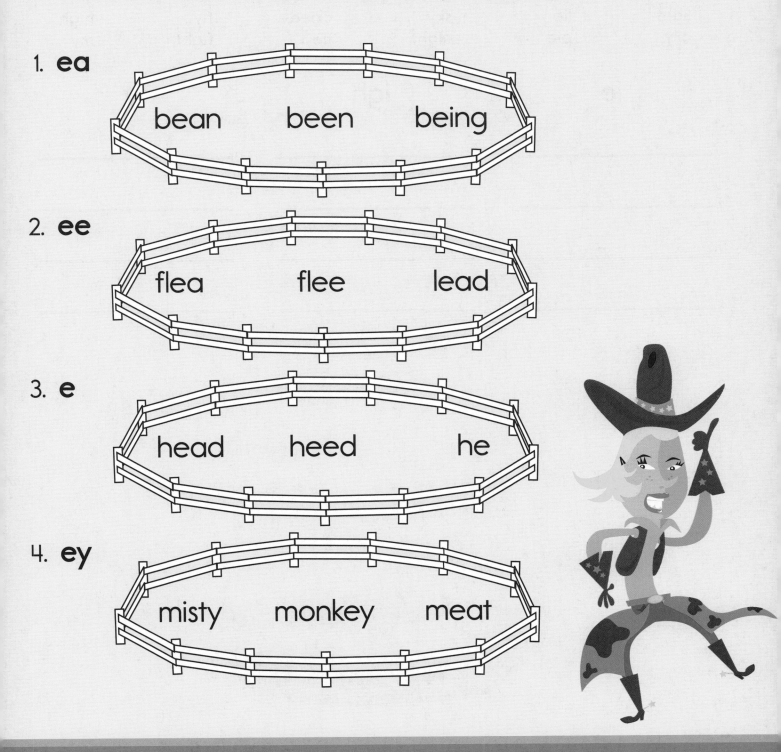

1. **ea**

bean   been   being

2. **ee**

flea   flee   lead

3. **e**

head   heed   he

4. **ey**

misty   monkey   meat

33

Sort It Out

Long i can be spelled "ie," "igh," and "y." Listen for it in *die*, *tight*, and *July*.

SORT the words. PUT the words into the lists.

light	lie	sky	cried	fly	high
cry	pie	night	tie	fight	my

ie	igh	y
_____	_____	_____
_____	_____	_____
_____	_____	_____
_____	_____	_____

Sound Search

"I spy with my little eye a word with long i!"

READ the story. CIRCLE words with the long i sound. FILL IN the blanks with the words.

Chef Toasty cooked all night long to bake the perfect pie. Just as the sky grew light, he put it on a high shelf. "My delight," he sighed. Chef shooed away a fly. Then he lay down for a nap. But a sly fox sneaked in a window. He grabbed the treat and ran. "Alas," cried Chef.

Would he bake a new one? He could try.

_____ _____ _____

_____ _____ _____

_____ _____ _____

_____ _____ _____

Herd That Word

Oh, give me a home.... Cowgirl Roma goes where long **o** roams! It can be spelled "o," "oa," or "ow."

LOOK at the spelling of the long **o** sound next to each fence. READ the words inside the fence. CIRCLE the word that has the correct spelling of long **o**.

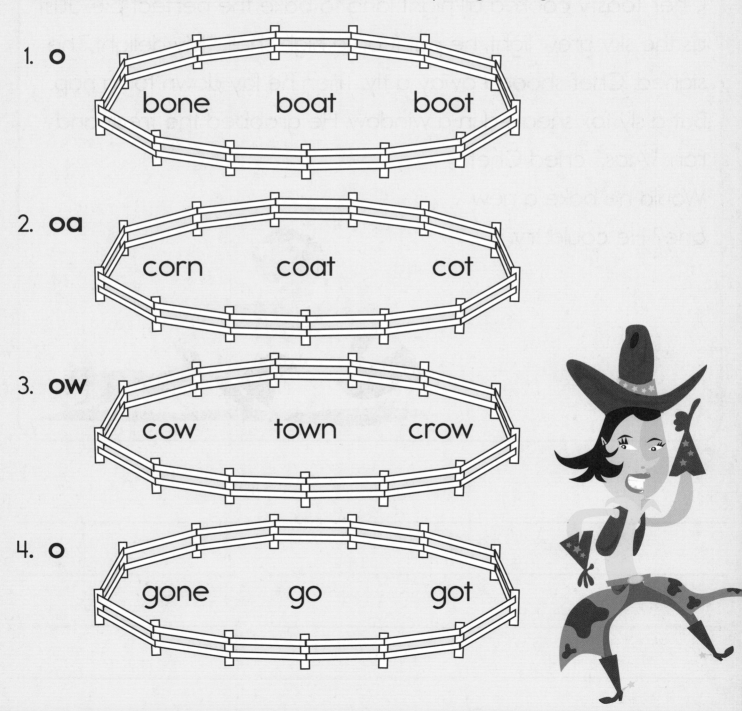

1. **o**

   bone   boat   boot

2. **oa**

   corn   coat   cot

3. **ow**

   cow   town   crow

4. **o**

   gone   go   got

Yo, Poet!

READ the poem. FILL IN the blanks with long **o** words from the word box.

gold	holes	toast	slow	cold
potatoes	boat	soap	cocoa	

Yo-ho-ho! Captain Moe

Sails the ocean in a _____.
₁

It leaks because it's full of _____.
₂

It's a wonder it can float.

It's stuffed with all his pirate loot—

Rubies, diamonds, silver, _____.
₃

It's very heavy and very _____.
₄

The water's also icy _____.
₅

"You know," says Moe, "I'd really like

To stay at home and drink _____,
₆

Wash with _____, grow _____,
₇ ₈

Butter _____, and play piano."
₉

What's This?

Hey, you! Long **u** can be spelled "u," "ew," "ue," and "ui." Examples are *music*, *chew*, *fuel*, and *fruit*.

LOOK at each picture. READ the words next to it. CIRCLE the correct word.

HINT: The correct word for each picture has a long **u**.

1. mule mole mill

2. stow stew stump

3. glow goo glue

4. just joust juice

Say Hey!

READ the sentences. FILL IN the blanks with long **u** words from the list.

HINT: The correct word rhymes with a word next to it.

| unicorn | knew | new | blue | juice | flu |

1. There are some red, some green, and a few

   _____.

2. The _____, you know, is worse than a really

   bad cold.

3. Some people think a _____ horn is magic.

4. Would you like some _____, Bruce?

5. The crew _____ it was time to take off.

6. I think I have discovered a

   _____ clue!

Build It

ADD a final "e" to each word. FILL IN the blanks with the new words.

1. can + e = _____

2. hug + e = _____

3. man + e = _____

4. mop + e = _____

5. not + e = _____

6. past + e = _____

7. rob + e = _____

8. slid + e = _____

Sort It Out

Shh! Some of these words have silent consonants. The rest do not.

SORT the words. PUT the words into the lists.

no	thumb	wrap	thump	knot	lamb
clump	know	not	write	rap	lamp

Words **with** Silent Consonants

_____

_____

_____

_____

_____

Words **without** Silent Consonants

_____

_____

_____

_____

_____

Herd That Word

Cowgirl Jen is after end-blends again! Help her rope them! LOOK at the blend next to each fence. READ the words inside the fence. CIRCLE the word that ends with the correct blend.

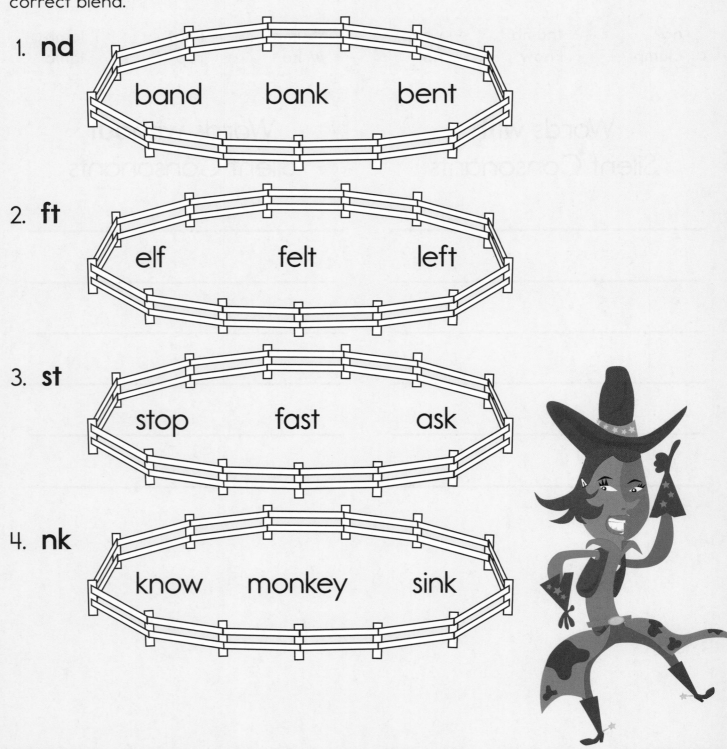

1. **nd**

band   bank   bent

2. **ft**

elf   felt   left

3. **st**

stop   fast   ask

4. **nk**

know   monkey   sink

Match the Socks

READ the words on the socks. MATCH each sock with another sock that contains a word with the same long vowel sound. COLOR the socks so they match.

HINT: Socks match if their words share the same long vowel sound, even if it is spelled differently.

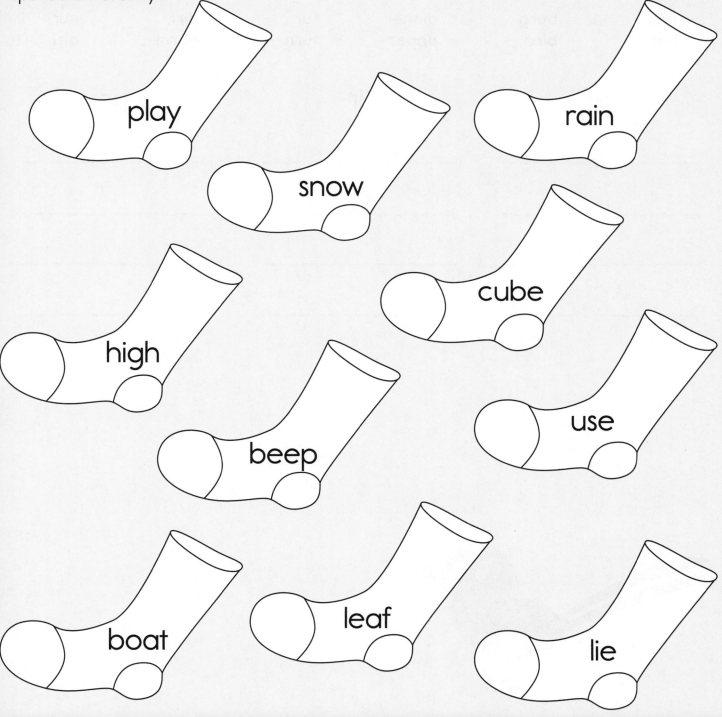

Because "R" Says So!

Sort It Out

The letter "r" is the boss of vowels. It changes their sounds. Check out bossy "r" at work in "er," "ir," and "ur," as in *her*, *fir*, and *blur*.

SORT the words. PUT the words into the lists. WRITE them on the blanks.

first	burp	dinner	fur	dirt	curl
herd	bird	paper	turn	germ	girl

er

_____

_____

_____

_____

ir

_____

_____

_____

_____

ur

_____

_____

_____

_____

Sound Search

Okay, detective. See if you can find the words with "er," "ir," and "ur" in them.

READ the story. CIRCLE words with the **r** sound. FILL IN the blanks with the words.

Bill the Bird invited Shelly the Turtle to dinner. He set the table with his best purple dishes and silver. Then he waited. And waited.

"Bad manners!" he thought when Shelly finally walked in—slowly. He stirred the soup.

"Ew, germs," thought Shelly, looking at her dirty dish. Suddenly a loud burp shook the table.

"Surprise!" said a voice. A spider popped up. "I ate first because it's my birthday."

_____ _____ _____

_____ _____ _____

_____ _____ _____

_____ _____ _____

Because "R" Says So!

What's This?

The letter "r" can make vowels say **or** even if they're spelled with an "ar," "or," "ore," or "our." Some examples are *wart*, *porch*, *more*, and *pour*.

LOOK AT each picture. READ the words next to it. CIRCLE the correct word.

1. weird   award   word

2. horse   hours   house

3. cork   chore   core

4. for   fur   four

Say Hey!

These sentences need words with bossy "r" in them.

READ the sentences. FILL IN the blanks with words from the list.

HINT: The correct word rhymes with a word next to it.

award	fork	wart	torn	bored	pour

1. I eat ham with a pork _____.

2. The jester did not make the _____ lord laugh.

3. Everyone loves her, so she won the Most Adored _____.

4. Please _____ four glasses of milk.

5. My old shirt is worn, _____, and dirty.

6. I named my dragon Snort-_____.

Because "R" Says So!

Herd That Word

The letter "r" makes "air," "are," and "ear" sound like **air** in many words, as in *fair*, *care*, and *tear*. Help Cowgirl Clair rope 'em!

LOOK at the spelling next to each fence. READ the words inside the fence. CIRCLE the word that has the correct spelling.

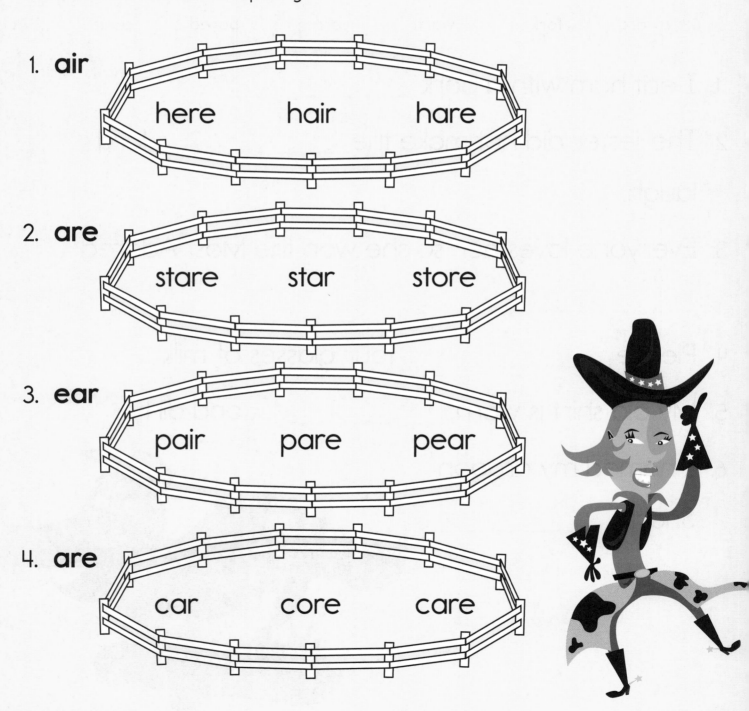

1. **air**

    here   hair   hare

2. **are**

    stare   star   store

3. **ear**

    pair   pare   pear

4. **are**

    car   core   care

Yo, Poet!

READ the poem. FILL IN the blanks with long **a** words from the list.

bear	stare	pair	care
hair	bare	fair	underwear

Fuzzy-wuzzy was a _____.
1

Fuzzy-wuzzy had no _____.
2

Other bears would stop and _____.
3

Fuzzy, he just didn't _____.
4

He had mittens—a nice red _____—
5

And toasty winter _____.
6

But still it isn't really _____
7

For a bear to be all _____.
8

Say Hey!

Sometimes letters just glide together to make a new vowel sound. The pairs "oi" and "oy," for example, make the sound **oy** as in *join* and *joy*.

READ the sentences. FILL IN the blanks with words from the word box.

HINT: The correct word rhymes with a word next to it.

> oyster   oil   boy   soil   toys   noise

1. Watch out for that kid—she destroys _____!

2. Be very careful when you boil _____.

3. A very wet shellfish is a moister _____.

4. Knock off all that _____, boys!

5. The queen's flowers grow in royal _____.

6. Is your cat a girl or a _____, Troy?

What's This?

Oy! Each picture here needs a label with the letters that glide together.

LOOK AT each picture. READ the words next to it. CIRCLE the correct word.

1. buy   boy   boil

2. nose   knees   noise

3. eel   oil   ail

4. toy   toil   toe

Herd That Word

Yow! Cowgirl Wow is out to pounce on "ou" and "ow"! Both spellings can sound like **ow**.

LOOK at the spelling of the **ow** sound next to each fence. READ the words inside the fence. CIRCLE the word that has the correct spelling.

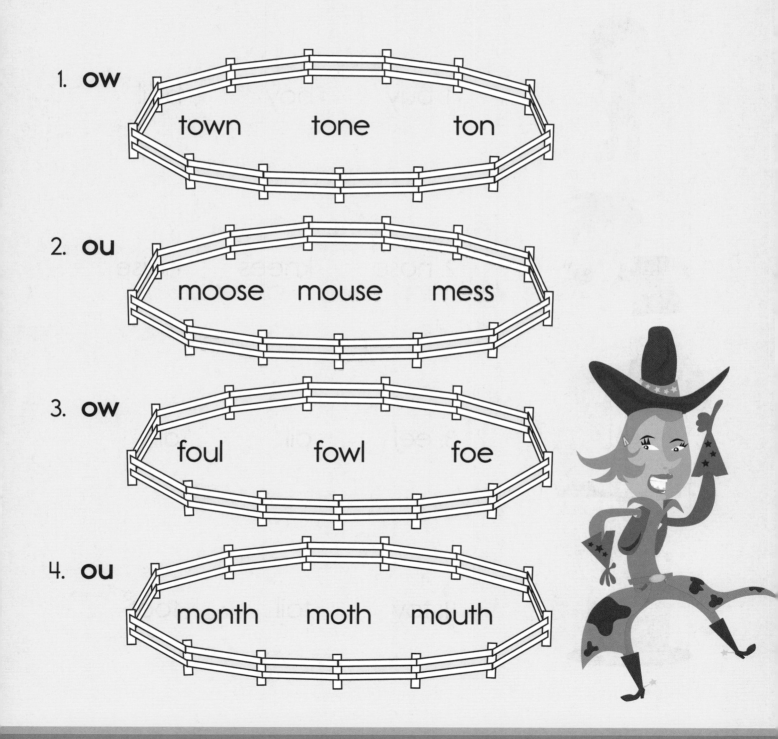

1. **ow**

   town   tone   ton

2. **ou**

   moose   mouse   mess

3. **ow**

   foul   fowl   foe

4. **ou**

   month   moth   mouth

Sound Search

READ the story. CIRCLE words that contain "ou" or "ow." FILL IN the blanks with the words.

"Wow!" said the brown hound dog as he looked at the fish in the fountain. "Look what I found. Trout!" His mouth watered. He crouched. Then he pounced. Splash!

"Help!" howled the dog. "I'm going to drown!"

Bess the Cow heard the loud sounds. So did Zeke the mouse. Together, they pulled the dog out.

"Stick to dog chow from now on," said Zeke.

_____   _____

_____   _____

_____   _____

_____   _____

_____   _____

_____   _____

_____   _____

Sort It Out

You go "moo" like a cow when you say the **oo** sound in *moon*. But "oo" can also sound like the **oo** in *book*. We'll call them the "Goo **oo**" and the "Good **oo**."

SORT the words. PUT the words into the lists.

hook	boot	food	look	poodle	cook
tooth	cool	wood	foot	school	took

Goo oo

_____

_____

_____

_____

_____

Good oo

_____

_____

_____

_____

_____

Yo, Poet!

READ the poem. FILL IN the blanks with **oo** words from the word box.

food	good	Shoo	zoo	moose
room	drool	books	zoom	goose

There is a creature in my _____.
₁

It likes to run and zip and _____.
₂

It has feathers like a _____
₃

And antlers like a big brown _____.
₄

You might think that this is cool.

But you should see it drip and _____!
₅

It gives me nasty, evil looks,

Eats my _____ and library _____.
₆   ₇

It doesn't smell _____. It belongs in a _____.
₈   ₉

But it won't go when I tell it, "_____!"
₁₀

What's This?

You can hear an **aw** sound in words spelled with "aw." But the "a" in "al" and "all" sometimes says **aw** too! Examples are *straw*, *walk*, and *wall*.

LOOK at each picture. READ the words next to it. CIRCLE the correct word.

1. bawl   ball   bale

2. yawn   yarn   yen

3. hank   hunk   hawk

4. chick   check   chalk

Say Hey!

Awww, each sentence is missing a word!

READ the sentences. FILL IN the blanks with words from the word box.

HINT: The correct word rhymes with a word next to it.

small   wall   claws   talk   bawl   dawn

1. All my baby sister does is crawl, _____, and sleep.

2. At _____, Fawn wakes up because she's an early riser.

3. Humpty-Dumpty had a bad fall off the tall _____.

4. You use a very _____ ball to play Ping-Pong.

5. I can walk, _____, and chew gum at the same time.

6. Who painted my cat's paws _____ red?

Herd That Word

Help Cowgirl Rhonda round up sounds! LOOK at the sound next to each fence. READ the words inside the fence. CIRCLE the word that has the right sound.

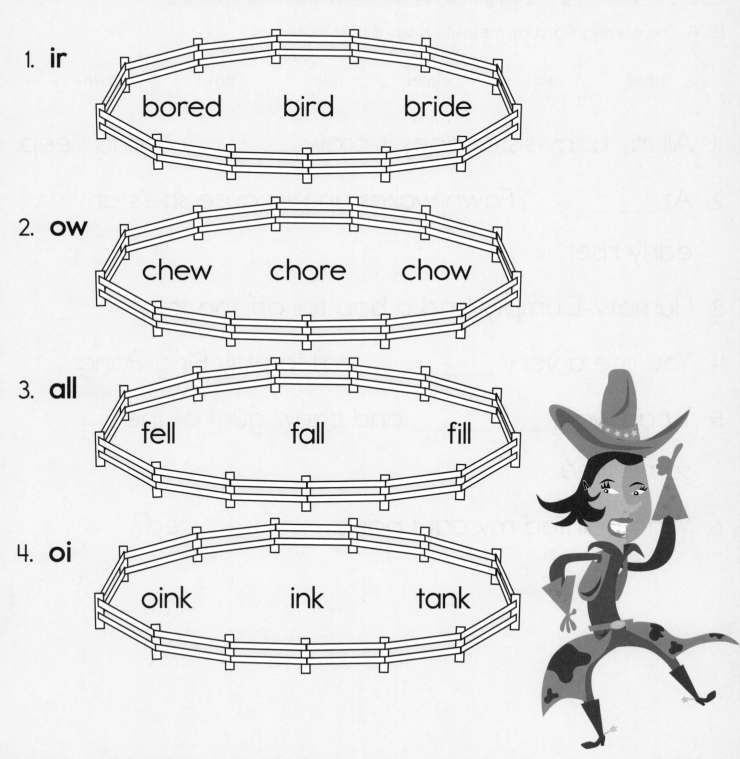

1. **ir**

bored   bird   bride

2. **ow**

chew   chore   chow

3. **all**

fell   fall   fill

4. **oi**

oink   ink   tank

Match the Socks

READ the words on the socks. MATCH each sock with another sock that contains a word with the same sound. COLOR the socks so they match.

HINT: Socks match if their words share the same sound, even if it is spelled differently.

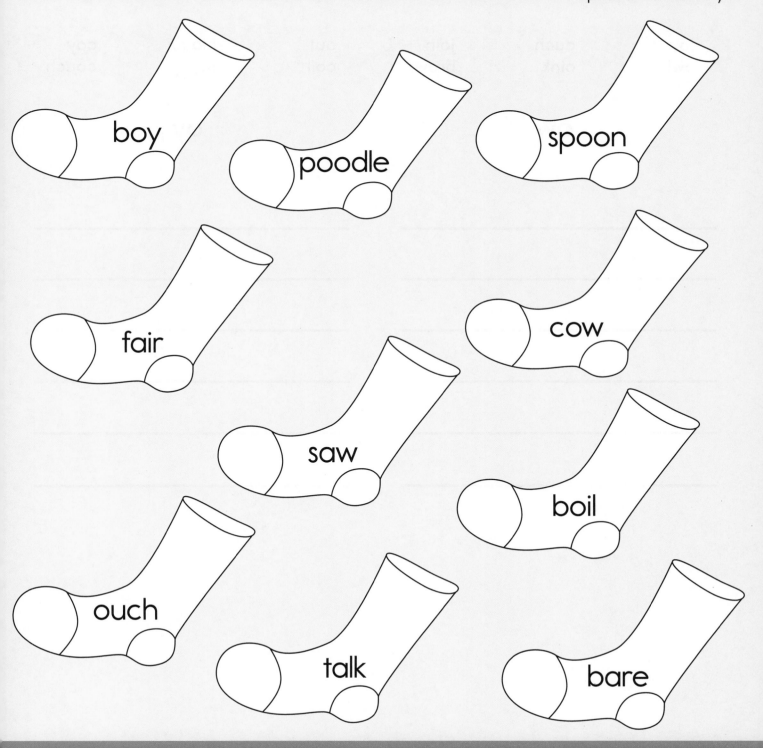

Sort It Out

SORT the words. PUT the words into the lists.

HINT: Listen for sounds in these words—and don't forget, different spellings can make the same sound!

| joy | ouch | join | out | cloud | coy |
| owl | oink | brown | coil | toy | couch |

ow

oy

_____ _____

_____ _____

_____ _____

_____ _____

_____ _____

What's This?

Uh-oh! Each picture needs a word with an **oo**.

LOOK at each picture. READ the words next to it. CIRCLE the correct word.

1. mouse   must   moose

2. buck   book   boot

3. spoon   spun   span

4. luck   look   lake

Compound Words

Build It

A **compound word** is a word that's made up of two words put together, like *notebook* and *toadstool*.

ADD each pair of words. FILL IN the blanks with the new compound words.

1. bull   + dog   = _____

2. snow   + man   = _____

3. black + berry = _____

4. cup   + cake   = _____

5. ginger + bread = _____

6. news   + paper = _____

7. pop   + corn   = _____

8. bath   + room   = _____

Break It Up

Split a compound word, and you get two words. *Firefighter*, for example, gives you *fire* and *fighter*. What a deal!

SPLIT each compound word. FILL IN the blanks with the two words.

1. daylight = _____ + _____

2. railroad = _____ + _____

3. toothbrush = _____ + _____

4. skateboard = _____ + _____

5. pinecone = _____ + _____

6. baseball = _____ + _____

7. suitcase = _____ + _____

8. starfish = _____ + _____

Compound Words

Match the Socks

READ the words on the socks. MATCH each sock with another sock to form a compund word. COLOR the socks so they match.

rattle

hopper

home

snake

straw

work

drop

rain

grass

berry

Blender Blunder

LOOK at the words in the blender. MATCH each word with a word in the list.
FILL IN the blanks with the correct words.

scare

butter

side

cup   jelly

tooth

1. _____ fish

2. _____ fly

3. _____ walk

4. _____ crow

5. _____ paste

6. _____ cake

Contractions

Build It

Speedy speaking means losing letters! Squash *I* and *am* together and you get *I'm*. *You* and *will* make *you'll*. *Do* plus *not* make *don't*. Words like this are called **contractions**.

READ the words. FILL IN the blanks with the correct contractions.

Example: you + are = you're

1. I   + will   = _____

2. we   + are   = _____

3. can + not   = _____

4. she + will   = _____

5. it   + is   = _____

6. you + have = _____

7. here + is   = _____

8. that + is   = _____

I'm done!

You've Got Mail

LOOK at the contractions in the word box. FILL IN the blanks with the right ones. You can use each contraction only once.

isn't	I'm	You're	wasn't	who's	what's
Here's	it's	she'll	she's	I'll	

_____ not going to believe me, but _____ true!
    ₁   ₂

My family is going to the moon! Seriously. _____ the
    ₃

plan: _____ going to build a rocket. Mom knows about
    ₄

engines, so _____ plan that. Guess _____ the
    ₅   ₆

pilot? My sister! I _____ going to bring her, but
    ₇

_____ the only driver. She says it _____ going
  ₈   ₉

to work. _____ show her! So, _____ up with you?
    ₁₀   ₁₁

Sort It Out

Pup is a word with one beat. *Puppy* has two beats. These beats are **syllables**. Most of the time, a syllable has a vowel in it.

COUNT the syllables in these words. SORT the words. PUT the words into the lists.

| somebody | princess | bib | machinery | wonderful | yank |
| seventeen | cookie | armadillo | troublemaker | monster | wise |

One Syllable

_____

_____

_____

Two Syllables

_____

_____

_____

Three Syllables

_____

_____

_____

Four Syllables

_____

_____

_____

Break It Up

SPLIT each word into syllables. FILL IN the blanks so that a dot sits between each syllable.

1. bulldozer = _____ • _____ • _____

2. crocodile = _____ • _____ • _____

3. fearful = _____ • _____

4. hamster = _____ • _____

5. Apatosaurus = ____ • ____ • ____ • ____ • ____

6. chipmunk = _____ • _____

7. Triceratops = ____ • ____ • ____ • ____

8. basketball = _____ • _____ • _____

Beat It!

Say Hey!

READ the sentences. FILL IN the blanks with words from the word box.

HINT: Each missing word rhymes with a word next to it—and also has the same number of syllables.

| mother | meter | battle | December | swallowing | alligator |

1. Put the dime in the parking _____, Peter.

2. The monster kept following, _____ people all the way!

3. Your lizard needs to take the _____ elevator.

4. Babies who fight are having a rattle _____.

5. My brother, _____, and father look just like me.

6. I can't remember _____ or January at all.

Herd That Word

Cowgirl Sybil's roping syllables—and she's counting on you!

LOOK at the number next to each fence. READ the words inside the fence. CIRCLE the word that has the correct number of syllables.

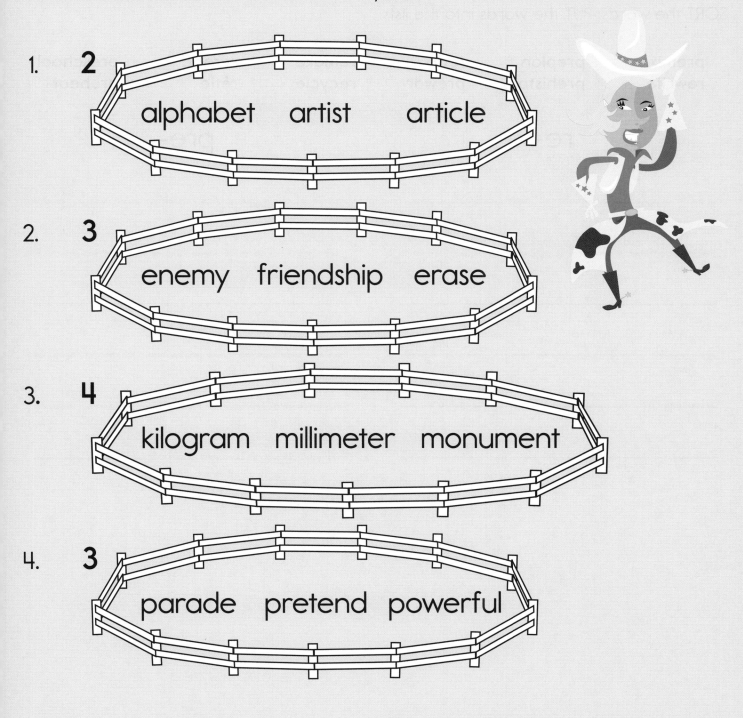

1. **2**
alphabet   artist   article

2. **3**
enemy   friendship   erase

3. **4**
kilogram   millimeter   monument

4. **3**
parade   pretend   powerful

Prefix Power

Sort It Out

A **prefix** is a letter or group of letters added to the beginning of a word. It changes a word's meaning. The prefix "re-," for example, means *back* or *again*. The prefix "pre-" means *before*. So *repay* means *pay back* but *prepay* means *pay before*.

SORT the words. PUT the words into the lists.

premix	preplan	redo	remake	reread	preschool
rewrite	prehistory	prewar	recycle	retie	preheat

re-

_____

_____

_____

_____

_____

pre-

_____

_____

_____

_____

_____

Break It Up

"Dis-" and "un-" swap a word's meaning! "Un-" turns *fair* into *unfair*. "Dis-" turns *respect* into *disrespect*. See what happens when you chop off these words' prefixes.

SPLIT each word. FILL IN the blanks with the prefix and the word.

1. unzip = _____ + _____

2. disagree = _____ + _____

3. disobey = _____ + _____

4. unreal = _____ + _____

5. disappear = _____ + _____

6. untie = _____ + _____

7. untidy = _____ + _____

8. dislike = _____ + _____

Prefix Power

Build It

It would be a mistake to diss "mis-"! The prefix "mis-" means *bad* or *wrong*.

ADD "mis-" to each word. FILL IN the blanks with the new words.

1. mis + use = _____

2. mis + treat = _____

3. mis + spell = _____

4. mis + lead = _____

5. mis + behave = _____

6. mis + match = _____

7. mis + place = _____

8. mis + understand = _____

Match the Socks

READ the socks. MATCH each sock with another sock. COLOR the socks so they match.

HINT: Socks with prefixes make pairs with socks that have words.

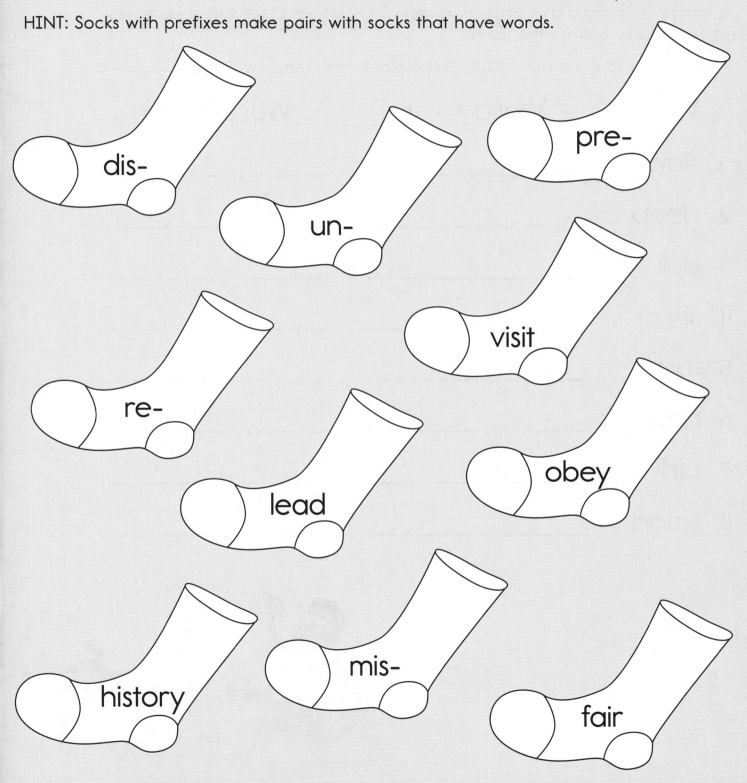

Build It

A **suffix** is a letter or group of letters added to the end of a word. A suffix can change a word's meaning a little or a lot. Adding "-er" or "-est," for example, makes *tall* even *taller* until it's the *tallest*.

ADD a suffix to each word. FILL IN the blanks with the new words.

Word	Word + -er	Word + -est
1. slow	_____	_____
2. deep	_____	_____
3. dull	_____	_____
4. short	_____	_____
5. fast	_____	_____
6. gross	_____	_____
7. old	_____	_____
8. smart	_____	_____

Build It

The suffix "-y" changes words so that they describe things. *Dust*, for example, turns into *dusty*. Its buddy "-ly" changes words so that they describe actions. *Glad*, for example, turns into *gladly*.

ADD each word to a suffix. FILL IN the blanks with the new words.

1. quick   + ly = _____

2. mess   + y = _____

3. twist   + y = _____

4. loud   + ly = _____

5. dead   + ly = _____

6. pick   + y = _____

7. strange + ly = _____

8. stink   + y = _____

Herd That Word

Sufferin' suffixes! Cowgirl Inga is at the end of her rope. She needs to round up words ending with the suffixes "-ed" and "-ing," as in *worked* and *working*.

LOOK at the suffix next to each fence. READ the words inside the fence. CIRCLE the word with the suffix on its end.

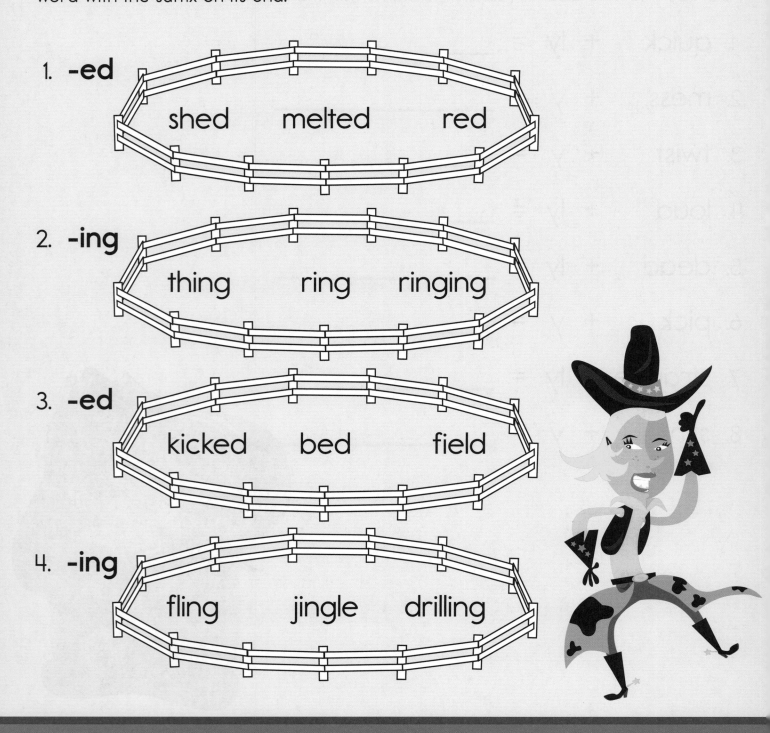

1. **-ed**

   shed   melted   red

2. **-ing**

   thing   ring   ringing

3. **-ed**

   kicked   bed   field

4. **-ing**

   fling   jingle   drilling

You've Got Mail

LOOK at the suffixes in the word box. FILL IN the blanks with the right suffixes. You can use suffixes more than once.

-er	-est	-ed	-ing	-y	-ly

Today will be the weird_____ day ever. We're visit_____

Aunt Rose. She has a very stink_____ pig for a pet. Last time

it chew_____ on my foot. Uncle Al is meet_____ us there.

He's even weird_____ than Aunt Rose. He lives in the world's

dark_____ house. It's creep_____ and awful_____ cold,

too! Strange_____, he hasn't turn_____ on the heat since

1969. Just think_____ about it makes me feel cold_____.

Match the Socks

READ the socks. MATCH each sock with another sock. COLOR the socks so they match.

HINT: Socks match if they make a word when they're put together.

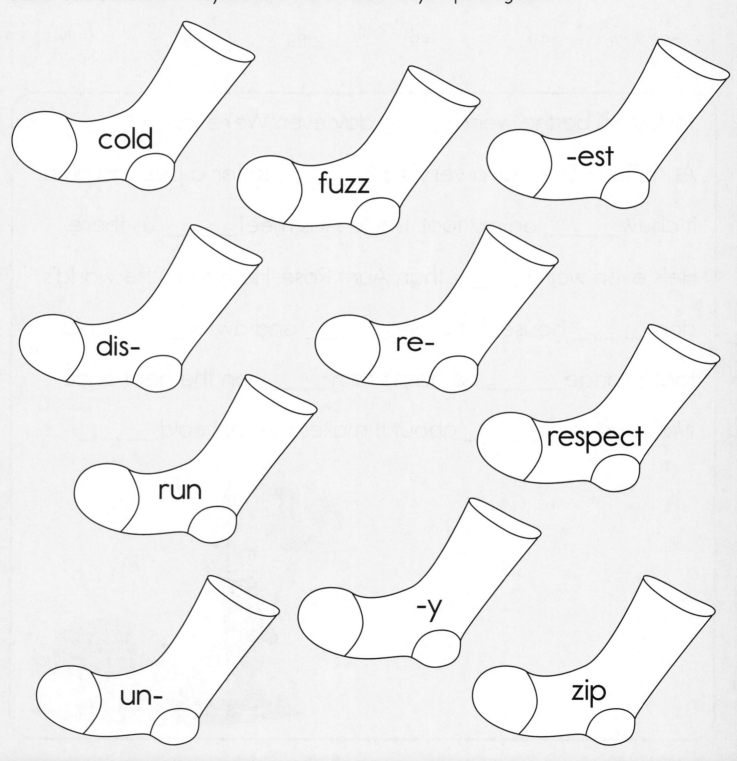

Build It

ADD the words and suffixes. FILL IN the blanks with the new words.

1. rest + ing = _____

2. glad + ly = _____

3. blue + bird = _____

4. day + dream = _____

5. pre + heat = _____

6. mis + spell = _____

7. itch + y = _____

8. sick + est = _____

Break It Up

Expand the contractions! SPLIT each contraction. FILL IN the blanks with the two words.

HINT: Get rid of the apostrophes and look for places to put *are*, *have*, *is*, *not*, and *will*.

Example: you're = you + are

1. can't   = _____ + _____

2. she'll   = _____ + _____

3. they're = _____ + _____

4. here's   = _____ + _____

5. we've   = _____ + _____

6. I'll   = _____ + _____

7. didn't   = _____ + _____

8. it's   = _____ + _____

Blender Blunder

LOOK at the words in the blender. MATCH each word with a word in the list.
FILL IN the blanks with the correct words.

police
basket
news
blue
shoe
thunder

1. _____ paper

2. _____ storm

3. _____ ball

4. _____ maker

5. _____ man

6. _____ berry

What's It About?

Pick the One!

A nonfiction book or article gives you lots of information about something. That "something" is the **main idea**.

LOOK at each book cover. READ the main ideas listed next to it. CIRCLE the correct main idea.

1.

   a. How balloons are made

   b. How to make balloon animals

   c. Why animals need air

2.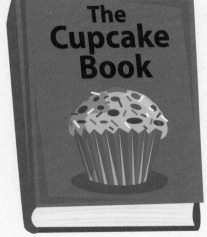

   a. How to bake cupcakes

   b. How to bake anything

   c. Foods of the world

3.

a. How to surf in the sea

b. How to make nets

c. How to use the Internet

4.

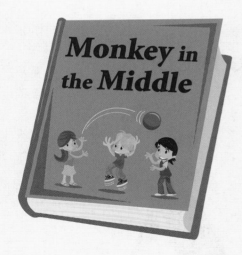

a. How to care for your monkey

b. Fun backyard games

c. How to start a zoo

What's the Big Idea?

A book has a main idea. So do smaller bits of writing—even paragraphs!

READ each paragraph. CIRCLE the sentence that sums up its main idea.

1. Do you like to slide on ice? Then you might like the sport of curling. The playing pieces are heavy pots called stones. The players slide the stones across the ice. They clear the stone's path by sweeping the ice with little brooms! They try to get their stones close to a target. The team with the most stones close to the target wins.

What's the main idea?

a. Sliding on ice will curl your hair.

b. Some people sweep ice with little brooms.

c. Curling is a sport played on ice.

2. | What kind of bird is a Roc? A Roc looks like a giant eagle—really giant! It's so big, it can pick up ships with its beak. It also likes to drop huge rocks on them. This big bird eats elephants for lunch. Its eggs are as big as a house. Luckily, you won't find it in your backyard! The Roc is found only in old stories.

What's the main idea?

a. Some birds lay eggs as big as houses.

b. The Roc is a very big, strong bird.

c. Old stories are scary.

Sort It Out

Main ideas are fine, but they need **supporting details** or you won't learn much. Check out these details. Which main ideas do they support?

SORT the words. PUT the words into the lists.

| pedals | bat | umpire | collar | mitt | tail |
| leash | brakes | barking | kickstand | pitcher | tires |

All About Dogs

_____

_____

_____

_____

How to Play Baseball

_____

_____

_____

_____

Parts of a Bicycle

_____

_____

_____

_____

It's All in the Details

These two kids are writing reports. Both kids have main ideas ready to go. But they need help with the supporting details.

LOOK at each kid's main idea. READ the supporting details. CIRCLE the details that support each kid's main idea. CROSS OUT the ones that don't.

1. Making Cool Flip-Flops

   a. Add flowers.

   b. Glue on glitter.

   c. Socks keep your feet warm.

   d. Color them with markers.

   e. It's fun to paint your toenails.

2. Caring for a Pet Rat

   a. Rats eat cheese.

   b. Owls eat mice.

   c. Rats like to hide.

   d. "Rat" spelled backward is "tar."

   e. You can teach rats tricks.

Teamwork Rules!

READ the paragraph. FILL IN the main idea and details.

People in every country like snacks—but they like different kinds. Some people in Cambodia enjoy fried spiders. Squid-flavored potato chips are a hit in Thailand. Some Canadians snack on crispy seaweed. Roasted ants are yummy in parts of South America. Think these snacks are weird? Try an American favorite—pieces of fried pigskin called pork rinds!

What is the main idea?

_____

_____

List the details.

1. _____   3. _____

2. _____   4. _____

5. _____

Volcanoes make many different kinds of lava. Lava that flows like a river full of sharp chunks of rock is called *aa*. Thin lava that flows fast and far is called *pahoehoe*. Volcanoes also spit out round blobs of lava called bombs. Blobs that are more like boxes are called blocks. Little lava stones are called *lapilli*.

What is the main idea?

_____

_____

List the details.

1. _____   3. _____

2. _____   5. _____

4. _____

Fix-up Mix-up

It's hard to understand what you read if it's all mixed up. The information has to be in the right order. That goes for fiction as well as nonfiction. This correct order is called **sequence**.

LOOK at the sentences and pictures. MATCH the sentences with pictures to put them in the right order.

1.

| Then add yogurt. | Mix them to make a smoothie. | First, put a banana into the blender. |

2.

| A baby bird hatched from the egg. | It laid an egg in the nest. | The bird built a nest. |

3. Mom gave
   me one.

I asked for
a haircut.

I'll never ask for
a haircut again!

4. Oops—
   it broke!

What a
big mess.

Zoe tied
the garbage
bag shut.

Order Up

Some words help you figure out sequence. Words like *first, next,* and *later* help you put things in order. You'll need them to understand this e-mail!

READ the paragraph. LOOK for the words in the word box. PUT the sentences in the right order and FILL IN the blanks.

first	next	then	after

> After the ride, I fed him some hay. First, I put a saddle on Blaze.
> Then, we went over the last jump. Next, I rode into the ring.

1. _____.

2. _____.

3. _____.

4. _____.

Order Up

Now try it with a newspaper article.

READ the article. LOOK for the words in the word box. PUT the sentences in the right order and FILL IN the blanks.

| after | finally | first | later | next | then |

Rocket Lands on Mars!

After passing the clouds, it zoomed into space. Later, it will leave Mars and go to Jupiter. First, the rocket's engines started. Next, it zipped past the clouds. Finally, it reached Mars. Then the rocket blasted off.

---

1. _____.

2. _____.

3. _____.

4. _____.

5. _____.

6. _____.

Make a Prediction

Pick the One!

When you think you know what is going to happen, you are making a **prediction**. You can look at a book and **predict** what it's going to be about.

LOOK at the book covers. CIRCLE the prediction that is the best match for each one.

1.

   a. This book tells you how to drive a car.
   b. This book is about a person who is a clown.
   c. This book is about circus elephants.

2.

   a. Dudley gets a great report card.
   b. Dudley teaches you how to play the kazoo.
   c. Everything goes wrong for Dudley.

3.

a. Kia's baseball broke the window. How will she pay for it?

b. Kia hits a record number of home runs! She's the star of Little League!

c. A window fell out of a house and landed right on Kia's baseball!

4.

a. This book is about all the things you can use to stick stuff together.

b. This book is all about bubblegum.

c. This book is about a boy who gets in trouble for chewing gum in class.

Make a Prediction

What Happens Next?

You can also use your powers of prediction after you start reading a book! READ the story starters. FILL IN the blanks with your predictions.

HINT: Ask yourself, "What happens next?"

1. The police dog sniffed the ground as he ran. He never took his nose off the trail. He was like a vacuum cleaner with legs! Suddenly he stopped. He sniffed harder. Then he began to dig. "What did you find, Sherlock?" said Officer Mya.

Prediction: _____

_____

2. Raj heard his cell phone ring. He pulled it out of his pocket. "Hello?" he said. But all he heard was a strange buzzing sound. It grew louder and louder. Then the phone began to shake. It shook so hard, Raj had to let go. The phone shot up into the air—and was sucked into the window of a UFO!

Prediction: _____

_____

3. Count von Looby heated a test tube over a flame. He wrote notes in his notebook. Then he emptied the test tube into a bowl. Sparks flew. A huge cloud of steam filled the air. "Hooray!" he cried, jumping up and down. "It worked! This discovery will change the world!" Just then, he heard a tap at his door.

Prediction: _____

_____

4. The fishermen leaned over the side of the boat. They grabbed the net and pulled with all their might. Finally, they got the net on board. It was full of fish. "What a great catch," said Hal.

    "Sure is," said Clyde. "But wait, what's this?"

    Hal and Clyde looked closer. Then Hal screamed, "Watch out!"

Prediction: _____

_____

Picture This!

You see pictures when you read—even if there are no pictures in the book! That's because you form pictures in your mind. You **visualize** what you're reading.

READ each sentence. CIRCLE the picture that matches it best.

1. The pirate opened the treasure chest, which was filled with gold!

a.　　　　　b.　　　　　c.

2. A wolf uses her mouth to pick up and carry her cub.

a.　　　　　b.　　　　　c.

3. Molly's new dress was long and covered with pink dots.

a.

b.

c.

4. Baby Bear was sad because someone ate his porridge.

a.

b.

c.

Use Your Doodle

You can put the picture in your mind on paper too!

READ each paragraph. DRAW the picture that it makes you visualize.

Everybody knows Australia has kangaroos. But Australia has other strange animals too. One of them is the numbat. It looks like a red squirrel with a long nose and white stripes on its body.

The hairy-nosed wombat is bigger. It looks like a cute, cuddly bear cub crossed with a pig. The quoll looks like a dark brown weasel covered with white spots. Strangest of all is the platypus. It's a furry brown animal with a tail like a beaver's and a bill like a duck's!

The strong wind snatched Jacob's hat off his head. Tumbleweeds raced by. His dog ran in circles around him, barking. "Come on, Chip," he called to the dog. He ducked his head and ran toward the house.

In the distance, he saw the tornado touch the ground. He knew it would reach the farm in less than a minute. Reaching down, he grabbed Chip's collar. He pushed the dog into the storm cellar. Then he jumped in too and pulled the door shut behind him.

Classify This!

Fiction or Not?

Okay, so you can predict what's in a book. You can visualize as you read. It's also important to **classify** what you're reading. You classify it when you decide that it is fiction or nonfiction. Remember: Fiction is made up. Nonfiction is all about facts.

LOOK at the book descriptions. READ the sentences. CLASSIFY the book. CIRCLE your answer.

In *Battle the Sea*, ten-year-old Yin tries to swim across the English Channel. But when a storm hits, she is swept away. Lost at sea, Yin fears she is doomed. Suddenly a seal rescues her. Where will the seal take her? Will she ever see her family again?

---

1. I think this book is: fiction   nonfiction

Knit Now tells you what you need to know to knit. Find out how to pick the right needles. Learn about different kinds of yarn. See how many different things you can make. Soon you'll be knitting scarves and mittens for your friends!

---

2. I think this book is: fiction   nonfiction

Clouds of Dust tells the story of a sad time in American history called the Dust Bowl. In the 1930s, land in part of the United States did not get a lot of rain.
The soil dried up and blew away.
Huge clouds of dust turned
the sky black.

3. I think this book is: fiction   nonfiction

Strike One for Cody is the story of Cody Walsh. He's always been the best hitter on the team. But now he's striking out all the time. Not only that, but he told a lie to his best friend Trey—and now Trey's not talking to him.

4. I think this book is: fiction   nonfiction

Classify This!

Sort It Out

Use your prediction skills to classify these book titles.

SORT the titles. PUT them into the lists.

The Cross-eyed Croc	How to Speak French
Be a Babysitter	Tessa's First Sleepover
Peppy Pup and Kitty Kit	All about Tape
Baking for Beginners	Mystery in the Ballpark

I Predict ... Fiction!

_____

_____

_____

I Predict ... Nonfiction!

_____

_____

_____

Match Up

Librarians classify books all the time. Books that are like each other are put into the same group.

LOOK at the list. CLASSIFY the books by drawing a line from each book to the name of a group.

American fiction

Music

Animals

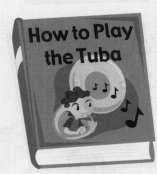

Math

That's Your Opinion

"Slugs are slimy" is a **fact**. "Slugs are yucky" is an **opinion**. It tells how you feel about the fact that slugs are slimy.

READ the sentences these kids are saying. CIRCLE the facts. UNDERLINE the opinions.

Broccoli is good for you.

Rain boots keep your feet dry.

Electricity is dangerous.

My mom is very strict.

I have a little sister.

Spinach is gross.

Your hair looks funny.

Sneakers are the best shoes in the world.

Herd Those Words

Cowgirl Shirl is after the truth. She wants facts, not opinions!

READ the sentences. CIRCLE the sentence that states a fact.

1. a. Cats are dumb.

    b. Cats have fur.

    c. Cats are the cutest animals.

2. a. Plums are purple.

    b. Purple is an ugly color.

    c. Purple is very cool.

3. a. Football is boring.

    b. Football is a sport.

    c. Football is exciting.

4. a. This soup is awful.

    b. This soup is delicious.

    c. This soup is tomato.

Sort It Out

Writers often use both facts and opinions. See if you can sort them out.

READ the paragraphs. FIND four facts and four opinions. WRITE them in the blanks.

The mayor is putting a new statue in the park. This is a bad idea. It will cost one million dollars. I think that money should be used to fix streets. The streets are full of cracks and potholes. Plus, the statue is really ugly. It's a giant troll. It'll look really bad!

Facts

_____

_____

_____

Opinions

_____

_____

_____

Sort It Out

Let's try another.

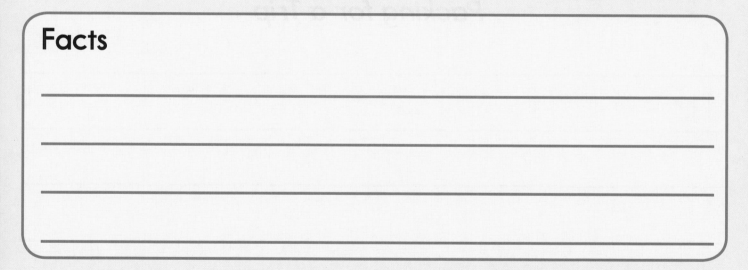

A new restaurant opened. We ate there yesterday. It wasn't very good. The hamburgers were really tasty. But the fries were too greasy. And the waiter was rude. They also sell milkshakes. I did not try one.

Facts

_____

_____

_____

_____

Opinions

_____

_____

_____

_____

Sort It Out

Look in the front of a book, and you may find a **table of contents.** The table of contents tells you what's in the book. It includes chapter titles and page numbers that show where chapters start. See if you can sort these chapter titles and put them with the right book.

SORT the titles. WRITE them on the blanks.

Buying a Suitcase	What Not to Bring
Side Dishes	Making the Sauce
What to Bring	The Best Pot to Use
How to Choose Noodles	Don't Forget Toothpaste

Packing for a Trip

_____

_____

_____

_____

Cooking Spaghetti

_____

_____

_____

_____

Look It Up

Take a look at this table of contents. Use it to answer the questions.

READ the questions. FILL IN the blanks.

1. What chapter tells about toy boats? _____

2. What chapter tells about blocks? _____

3. What chapter tells about radio-controlled planes?

_____

4. What chapter tells about toys from 100 years ago?

_____

What Do You Mean?

Some books have a mini dictionary in them. It's called a **glossary**. The glossary is at the end of the book. It gives you meanings for some words in the book. Try writing one here.

READ the words. FILL IN the blanks with a definition for each one.

A Glossary for *The Book of Food*

banana: _____

_____

carrot: _____

_____

doughnut: _____

_____

hot dog: _____

_____

lemon: _____

_____

Find It Fast

A nonfiction book may have an **index** at the very end. An index is a list of words in alphabetical order. You use it to look up a topic and find out what page it's on.

READ the sentences. LOOK UP the answers in the index. FILL IN the blanks with the page numbers.

1. "Bluebird" is on page _____.
2. "Nests" is on page _____.
3. "Woodpecker" is on page _____.
4. "Flight" is on page _____.
5. "Ovenbird" is on page _____.
6. "Crow" is on page _____.

Index for *The Book of Birds*

bluebird, 21

bluejay, 26

crow, 17

duck, 52

flight, 10

food, 8

goose, 43

nests, 9

ovenbird, 28

woodpecker, 33

wren, 40

As a Matter of Fact

READ the sentences the family is saying. CIRCLE the facts. DRAW A LINE under the opinions.

I think my bedtime is way too early.

It was sunny this morning.

Our class has a new teacher.

This food is disgusting.

The bus got a flat tire on the way to school.

Seth is the funniest person in the world.

Everything tastes better with yams in it.

The cat ate the canary today.

Blank Out

READ the book pages. FILL IN the blanks with words from the list.

glossary	index	table of contents

1. This book part is the _____.

fang: a long, sharp tooth
forked: a tongue that ends in two points
scale: thick patches in a snake's skin
venom: a snake's poison

2. This book part is the _____.

boa, 6
deserts, 24
eggs, 4
fangs, 8
rattlesnake, 13
sidewinder, 5
viper, 17

3. This book part is the _____.

Fiction or Not?

LOOK at the book covers. READ the sentences. CLASSIFY the book. CIRCLE your answer.

1.

Ty loves his pet turtle, Boo. Boo and Ty like to run races in slow motion in the yard. One sad day, Ty can't find Boo anywhere. He fears that Boo has run away. But why? Does Boo's disappearance have anything to do with the speedy rabbit next door?

I think this book is   fiction   nonfiction

2.

A turtle's body is protected by its shell. Many kinds of turtles can pull their heads, tails, and legs into their shells. The box turtle can even clamp its shell shut after it pulls everything in! This book tells you everything you want to know about turtles.

I think this book is   fiction   nonfiction

Page 2
br: break, bring, brave
cl: clam, clock, cloud
fl: flip, floppy, flower
gr: grape, green, ground
bl: black, block, blue

Page 3
1. blaze
2. crab
3. frown
4. please

Page 4
1. blouse
2. cloud
3. brave
4. drive
5. floor
6. triangle

Page 5
Wow! Today I flew down a **steep** hill on my **skateboard**. I went so fast the wheels made **smoke**. It was **sweet**! But I had to **slow** down and **spin** sideways when a **skunk** suddenly crawled across the street like a tired **snail** or else it would have made a big **stink**. **Scary**!

Page 6
1. crabby, crocodile, crayon→Craig
2. spot, spinach, spoon→Spencer
3. snack, snake, snowman→Snowden
4. frog, French, fries→Francis
5. troll, tractor, trouble→Trixie
6. Please, plant, plate→Placido

Page 7
France, sleep, creepy, dragon, prowled, crushed, claws, broke, branches, trees, breath, fried, grass, problem, tried, trap, prince, flew, scared, grinning, spider, ground, pretty, great

Page 8
A really **strange** thing happened today. I was eating a bowl of **strawberry** ice cream when I heard a loud **screech**. Then I heard a **squeak** and a **squawk**. I jumped up to look out the window and saw a noisy **struggle** going on between a **squirrel** and a bird. They were playing tug-of-war with a **string**! Suddenly the bird let go. The squirrel fell into the **stream** with a **splash**. I sat down in surprise. Whoops. I **squashed** my ice cream—and let out a **scream**!

Page 9
spr: spray, spread, spring
squ: square, squash, squirm
spl: split, splat, splash
scr: screech, scram, scream
str: strike, street, stripe

Page 10
1. shelf
2. jump
3. want
4. left

Page 11
1. wind, and, sand→Desmond
2. Honk, pink, tank→Hank
3. aunt, went, sent→Millicent
4. jump, ramp, swamp→Kemp
5. best, west, fast→Amethyst
6. Ask, task, tusk→Fisk

Page 12
1. breakfast
2. soft
3. sent
4. felt
5. sunk
6. swamp
Note: "sump" and "swank" are also possbile answers to 5 and 6.

Page 13
1. lamp
2. ant
3. desk
4. elf

Page 14
cr: creep, cry
st: sting, stone
scr: scratch, screech
str: street, string
nk: sink, junk
nd: sand, wind

Page 15

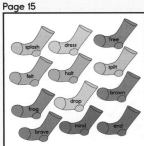

Page 16
1. She, shells, shore→Sheila
2. chubby, chicken, cheese→Chuck
3. think, thousand, things→Theo
4. white, whale, Whatever→Whitney
5. threw, three, through→Thrasher

Page 17
1. cheese
2. wheel
3. thunder
4. thread
5. shark

Page 18
1. laugh
2. thing
3. sting
4. cough

Page 19
1. rough
2. sting
3. laugh
4. song
5. rang
6. tough

Page 20
Hard c: cat, cave, cold, cobwebs, canary
Soft c: Cinnamon, ceiling, Centipedes, center, circle

Page 21

Page 22
Hard g: gab, goat, girl, game, garden, gobble
Soft g: gentle, general, germ, ginger, giraffe, giant

Page 23
1. gorilla
2. gym
3. gift
4. ginger

Page 24
kn: knees, know
wr: wrong, wreck
mb: crumb, lamb

Page 25
1. knight
2. comb
3. writer
4. knee

Page 26

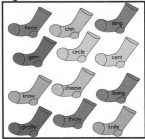

Page 27
1. goofy, goat, gear→Gordon
2. can't, carry, camel→Carl
3. Wrap, write, wrong→Wren
4. shark, sharp, shy→Shelby
5. cough, laugh, enough→Hough
6. circus, Centipede City→Cindy

Page 28
1. cute
2. dime
3. fine
4. fire
5. kite
6. made
7. pine
8. plane

Page 29
mole, nose, fine, came, hate, shade, pine, lake, shape, plane, kite, time, hide, dive, hole, rude, mule, joke

Page 30
1. gray
2. play
3. way
4. rain
5. pain
6. jail
7. wail
8. pails
9. eight

Page 31

Page 32
1. seal
2. me
3. neat
4. sheep
5. honey
6. sneak

Page 33
1. bean
2. flee
3. he
4. monkey

Page 34
ie: lie, cried, pie, tie
igh: light, high, night, fight
y: sky, fly, cry, my

Page 35
night, pie, sky, light, high, my, delight, sighed, fly, sly, cried, try

Page 36
1. bone
2. coat
3. crow
4. go

Answers

Page 37
1. boat
2. holes
3. gold
4. slow
5. cold
6. cocoa
7. soap
8. potatoes
9. toast

Page 38
1. mule
2. stew
3. glue
4. juice

Page 39
1. blue
2. flu
3. unicorn
4. juice
5. knew
6. new

Page 40
1. cane
2. huge
3. mane
4. mope
5. note
6. paste
7. robe
8. slide

Page 41
Silent Consonants: knot, know, lamb, thumb, wrap, write
Without Silent Consonants: not, no, lamp, thump, rap, clump

Page 42
1. band
2. left
3. fast
4. sink

Page 43
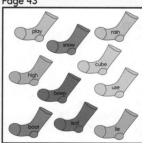

Page 44
er: dinner, germ, herd, paper
ir: bird, dirt, first, girl
ur: burp, curl, fur, turn

Page 45
Bird, Turtle, dinner, purple, silver, manners, stirred, germs, her, dirty, burp, Surprise, spider, first, birthday

Page 46
1. award
2. horse
3. core
4. four

Page 47
1. fork
2. bored
3. award
4. pour
5. torn
6. wart

Page 48
1. hair
2. stare
3. pear
4. care

Page 49
1. bear
2. hair
3. stare
4. care
5. pair
6. underwear
7. fair
8. bare

Page 50
1. toys
2. oil
3. oyster
4. noise
5. soil
6. boy

Page 51
1. boy
2. noise
3. oil
4. toy

Page 52
1. town
2. mouse
3. fowl
4. mouth

Page 53
Wow, brown, hound, fountain, found, Trout, mouth, crouched, pounced, howled, drown, Cow, loud, sounds, mouse, out, chow, now

Page 54
Goo oo: boot, cool, food, poodle, school, tooth
Good oo: cook, foot, wood, hook, look, took

Page 55
1. room
2. zoom
3. goose
4. moose
5. drool
6. food
7. books
8. good
9. zoo
10. Shoo

Page 56
1. ball
2. yawn
3. hawk
4. chalk

Page 57
1. bawl
2. dawn
3. wall
4. small
5. talk
6. claws

Page 58
1. bird
2. chow
3. fall
4. oink

Page 59
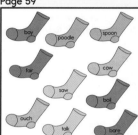

Page 60
ow: brown, cloud, ouch, out, owl, couch
oy: coy, coil, join, joy, toy, oink

Page 61
1. moose
2. book
3. spoon
4. look

Page 62
1. bulldog
2. snowman
3. blackberry
4. cupcake
5. gingerbread
6. newspaper
7. popcorn
8. bathroom

Page 63
1. day + light
2. rail + road
3. tooth + brush
4. skate + board
5. pine + cone
6. base + ball
7. suit + case
8. star + fish

Page 64
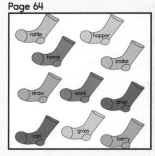

Page 65
1. jellyfish
2. butterfly
3. sidewalk
4. scarecrow
5. toothpaste
6. cupcake

Page 66
1. I'll
2. we're
3. can't
4. she'll
5. it's
6. you've
7. here's
8. that's

Page 67
1. You're
2. it's
3. Here's
4. I'm
5. she'll
6. who's
7. wasn't
8. she's
9. isn't
10. I'll
11. what's

Page 68
One Syllable: bib, wise, yank
Two Syllables: cookie, monster, princess
Three Syllables: seventeen, somebody, wonderful
Four Syllables: armadillo, machinery, troublemaker

Page 69
1. bull · doz · er
2. croc · o · dile
3. fear · ful
4. ham · ster
5. A · pat · o · saur · us
6. chip · munk
7. Tri · cer · a · tops
8. bas · ket · ball

Page 70
1. meter
2. swallowing
3. alligator
4. battle
5. mother
6. December

Answers

Page 71
1. artist
2. enemy
3. millimeter
4. powerful

Page 72
re-: recycle, redo, remake, reread, retie, rewrite
pre-: preheat, prehistory, premix, preplan, preschool, prewar

Page 73
1. un + zip
2. dis + agree
3. dis + obey
4. un + real
5. dis + appear
6. un + tie
7. un + tidy
8. dis + like

Page 74
1. misuse
2. mistreat
3. misspell
4. mislead
5. misbehave
6. mismatch
7. misplace
8. misunderstand

Page 75

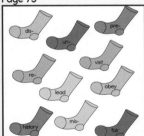

Page 76
1. slow slower slowest
2. deep deeper deepest
3. dull duller dullest
4. short shorter shortest
5. fast faster fastest
6. gross grosser grossest
7. old older oldest
8. smart smarter smartest

Page 77
1. quickly
2. messy
3. twisty
4. loudly
5. deadly
6. picky
7. strangely
8. stinky

Page 78
1. melted
2. ringing
3. kicked
4. drilling

Page 79
Today will be the **weirdest** day ever. We're **visiting** Aunt Rose. She has a very **stinky** pig for a pet. Last time it **chewed** on my foot. Uncle Al is **meeting** us there. He's even **weirder** than Aunt Rose. He lives in the world's **darkest** house. It's **creepy** and **awfully** cold, too! **Strangely,** he hasn't **turned** on the heat since 1969. Just **thinking** about it makes me feel **colder.**

Page 80

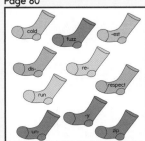

Page 81
1. resting
2. gladly
3. bluebird
4. daydream
5. preheat
6. misspell
7. itchy
8. sickest

Page 82
1. can + not
2. she + will
3. they + are
4. here + is
5. we + have
6. I + will
7. did + not
8. it + is

Page 83
1. newspaper
2. thunderstorm
3. basketball
4. shoemaker
5. policeman
6. blueberry

Pages 84–85
1. b
2. a
3. c
4. b

Pages 86–87
1. c
2. b

Page 88
All About Dogs: collar, tail, leash, barking
How to Play Baseball: bat, mitt, umpire, pitcher
Parts of a Bicycle: pedals, tires, brakes, kickstand

Page 89
1. Making Cool Flip-Flops
   a. Add flowers.
   b. Glue on glitter.
   c. Socks keep your feet warm.
   d. Color them with markers.
   e. It's fun to paint your toenails.

2. Caring for a Pet Rat
   a. Rats eat cheese.
   b. Owls eat mice.
   c. Rats like to hide.
   d. "Rat" spelled backward is "tar."
   e. You can teach rats tricks.

Page 90
Suggestions:
Main Idea: People eat different snacks in different countries.
Details: 1. fried spiders, 2. squid-flavored potato chips, 3. seaweed, 4. roasted ants, 5. pork rinds

Page 91
Suggestions:
Main Idea: There are different kinds of lava.
Details: 1. aa, 2. pahoehoe, 3. bombs, 4. blocks, 5. lapilli

Page 92

Page 93

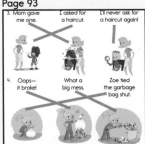

Page 94
1. First, I put a saddle on Blaze.
2. Next, I rode into the ring.
3. Then, we went over the last jump.
4. After the ride, I fed him some hay.

Page 95
1. First, the rocket's engines started.
2. Then the rocket blasted off.
3. Next, it zipped past the clouds.
4. After passing the clouds, it zoomed into space.
5. Finally, it reached Mars.
6. Later, it will leave Mars and go to Jupiter.

Pages 96–97
1. b
2. c
3. a
4. b

Pages 98–99
Suggestions:
1. Sherlock finds something that was dropped by the person he is tracking and will soon find the person.
2. Raj will be taken aboard the UFO and will meet space aliens.
3. Count von Looby will open the door and find his neighbor there, who asks him to please keep the noise down.
4. Hal and Clyde discover that they have caught a huge sea monster.

Pages 100–101
1. c
2. a
3. c
4. b

Pages 102–103
Be sure the pictures match something from the paragraphs.

Pages 104–105
1. fiction
2. nonfiction
3. nonfiction
4. fiction

Page 106
Fiction: The Cross-eyed Croc, Peppy Pup and Kitty Kit, Tessa's First Sleepover, Mystery in the Ballpark
Nonfiction: Be a Babysitter, Baking for Beginners, How to Speak French, All about Tape

Page 107

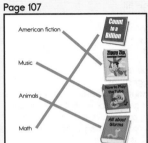

Answers

Page 108
Facts
Broccoli is good for you.
Rain boots keep your feet dry.
Electricity is dangerous.
I have a little sister.
Opinions
Spinach is gross.
Sneakers are the best shoes in the world.
Your hair looks funny.
My mom is very strict.

Page 109
1. b
2. a
3. b
4. c

Page 110
Facts
1. The mayor is putting a new statue in the park.
2. It will cost one million dollars.
3. The streets are full of cracks and potholes.
4. It's a giant troll.
Opinions
1. This is a bad idea.
2. I think that money should be used to fix streets.
3. Plus, the statue is really ugly.
4. It'll look really bad.

Page 111
Facts
1. A new restaurant opened.
2. We ate there yesterday.
3. They also sell milkshakes.
4. I did not try one.
Opinions
1. It wasn't very good.
2. The hamburgers were really tasty.
3. But the fries were too greasy.
4. And the waiter was rude.

Page 112
Packing for a Trip: Buying a Suitcase, What to Bring, What Not to Bring, Don't Forget Toothpaste
Cooking Spaghetti: How to Choose Noodles, Making the Sauce, The Best Pot to Use, Side Dishes

Page 113
1. 4
2. 6
3. 3
4. 1

Page 114
Suggestions:
Banana: long yellow fruit with a peel that gets black spots if you leave it lying around for too long
Carrot: an orange vegetable that rabbits like a lot
Doughnut: a circle of dough around a hole
Hot dog: meat shaped like a tube that you put mustard on
Lemon: a sour yellow fruit about the size of a baseball

Page 115
1. 21
2. 9
3. 33
4. 10
5. 28
6. 17

Page 116
Facts
It was sunny this morning.
Our class has a new teacher.
The cat ate the canary today.
The bus got a flat tire on the way to school.
Opinions
Seth is the funniest person in the world.
This food is disgusting.
I think my bedtime is way too early.
Everything tastes better with yams in it.

Page 117
1. table of contents
2. glossary
3. index

Page 118
1. fiction
2. nonfiction